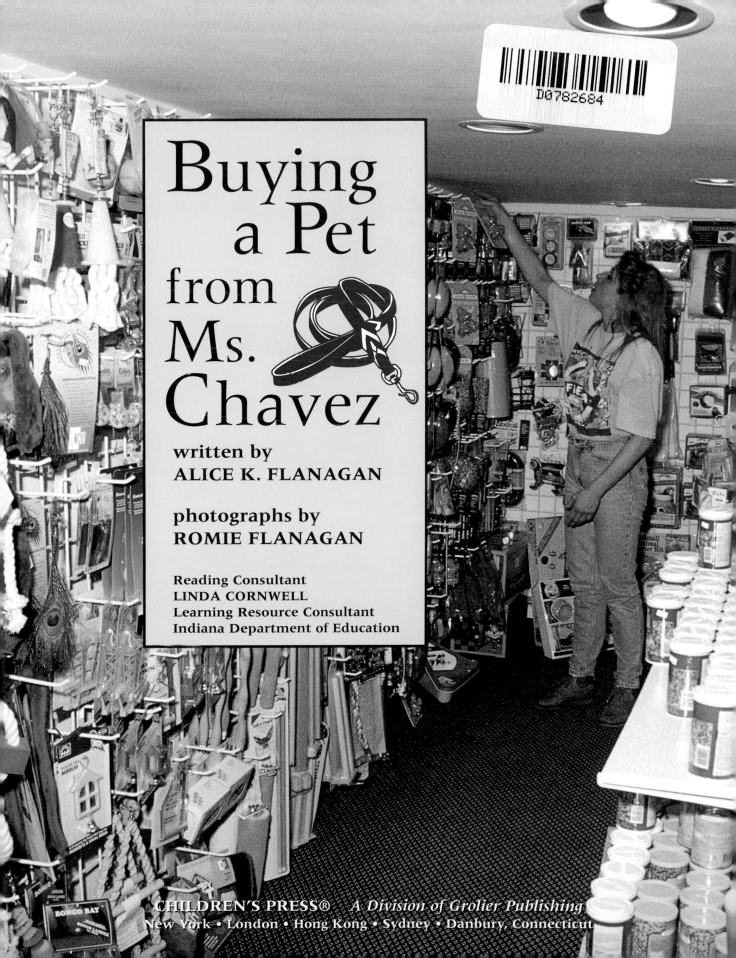

Buying a Pet from Ms. Chavez

written by
ALICE K. FLANAGAN

photographs by
ROMIE FLANAGAN

Reading Consultant
LINDA CORNWELL
Learning Resource Consultant
Indiana Department of Education

CHILDREN'S PRESS® A Division of Grolier Publishing
New York • London • Hong Kong • Sydney • Danbury, Connecticut

Special thanks to Catherine Chavez for allowing us to tell her story.

Also thanks to Collar and Leash Pet Store.

Author's Note:
Ms. Chavez's last name is pronounced SHA-vez.

Library of Congress Cataloging-in-Publication Data
Flanagan, Alice.
  Buying a pet from Ms. Chavez / written by Alice K. Flanagan ; photographs by Romie Flanagan ; reading consultant, Linda Cornwell.
    p.   cm. — (Our neighborhood)
  Summary: Text and photographs show what is involved in running a pet store: caring for the animals, helping customers, ordering supplies, and more.
    ISBN 0-516-20773-3 (lib.bdg.)   0-516-26293-9 (pbk.)
  1. Pets—Juvenile literature. 2. Pet shops—Juvenile literature. 3. Pets—Buying—Juvenile literature. [1. Pet shops. 2. Occupations.] I. Flanagan, Romie, ill. II. Title. III. Series: Our neighborhood (New York, N.Y.)
  SF416.2.F58   1998
  636.088'7—dc21
                                        97-11866
                                        CIP
                                        AC

Photographs ©: Romie Flanagan

Ms. Chavez loves animals. They are her friends.

Ever since she was a little girl,
Ms. Chavez has been caring for
animals. Now it is her job.

Ms. Chavez has been working in this pet store for nine years.

It's a very busy place. When the owner isn't there, Ms. Chavez is in charge.

She orders most of the food and supplies the animals need.

Then she stacks the shelves when the items come in.

Ms. Chavez helps the customers
and answers all of their questions.

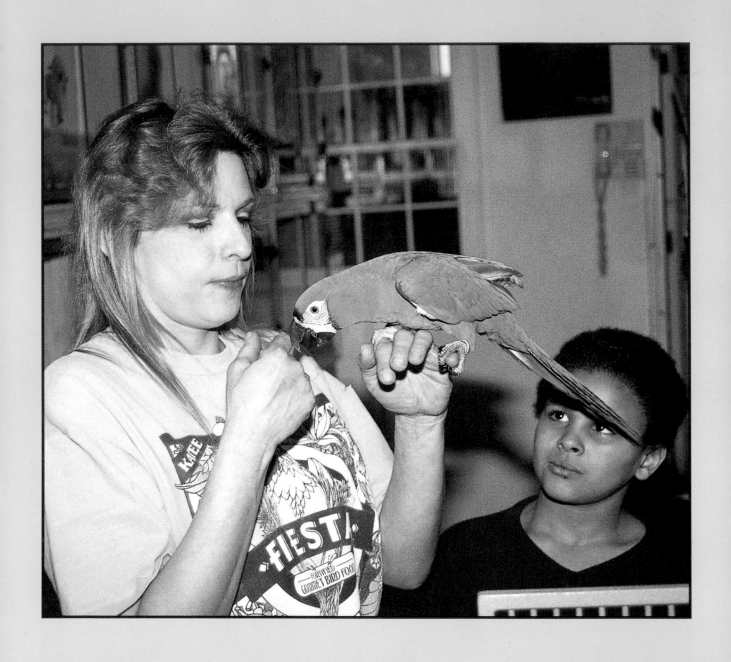

Every day, she helps them choose
pets to buy.

She talks to them about what the
animals need.

Sometimes, pet owners go out of town. They bring their pets to the pet store so Ms. Chavez can care for them.

Ms. Chavez makes sure that all the animals in the store stay healthy. Caring for so many animals is hard work.

Each animal needs something different.

Each one wants special attention.

Birds like to be talked to.

Dogs are happy when they're brushed.

Kittens purr when they're petted.

Fish like clean water and swim all day long.

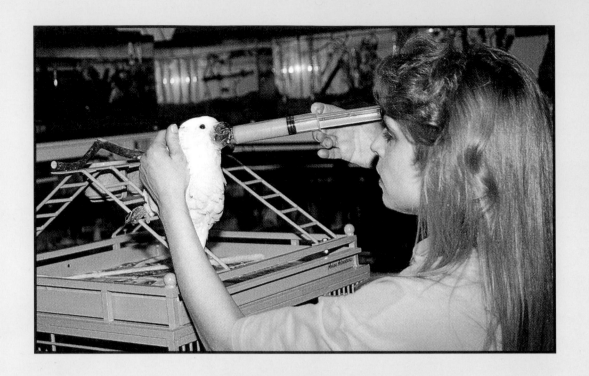

Every day, Ms. Chavez feeds the animals . . .

. . . and cleans up after them.

When an animal is sick, she gives it medicine.

If an animal is very sick, Ms. Chavez takes it to a doctor.

Pets keep people company and make them happy.

Ms. Chavez tries to keep the animals in her store happy, too.

Someday, she wants to raise dogs and cats on her own.

Ms. Chavez loves caring for animals and finding homes for them. There's nothing in life she enjoys doing as much!

Meet the Author and the Photographer

Alice and Romie Flanagan live in Chicago, Illinois, and have been involved in publishing for many years. Alice is a writer, and Romie is a photographer. As husband and wife, they enjoy working together closely. They hope their books help children learn about the people in their community and how their jobs affect the neighborhood.

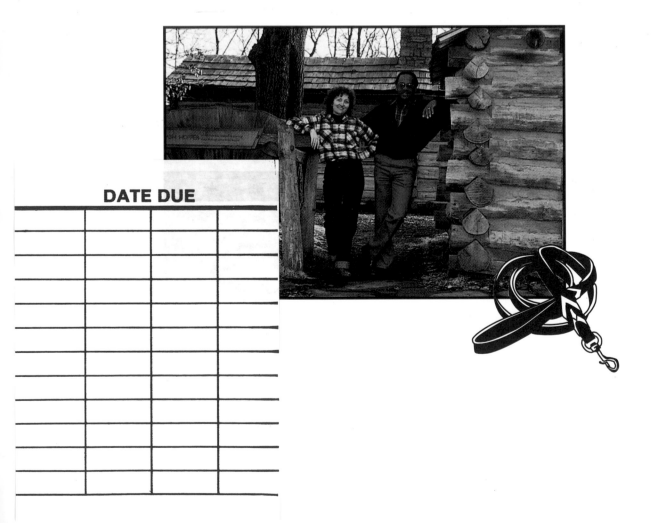